BRITNEY SPEARS

A Real-Life Reader Biography

Ann Graham Gaines

Mitchell Lane Publishers, Inc.
Bear, Delaware 19701

Third Printing

Real-Life Reader Biographies

Selena	Robert Rodriguez	Mariah Carey	Rafael Palmeiro
Tommy Nuñez	Trent Dimas	Cristina Saralegui	Andres Galarraga
Oscar De La Hoya	Gloria Estefan	Jimmy Smits	Mary Joe Fernandez
Cesar Chavez	Chuck Norris	Sinbad	Paula Abdul
Vanessa Williams	Celine Dion	Mia Hamm	Sammy Sosa
Brandy	Michelle Kwan	Rosie O'Donnell	Shania Twain
Garth Brooks	Jeff Gordon	Mark McGwire	Salma Hayek
Sheila E.	Hollywood Hogan	Ricky Martin	**Britney Spears**
Arnold Schwarzenegger	Jennifer Lopez	Kobe Bryant	Derek Jeter
Steve Jobs	Sandra Bullock	Julia Roberts	Robin Williams
Jennifer Love Hewitt	Keri Russell	Sarah Michelle Gellar	Liv Tyler
Melissa Joan Hart	Drew Barrymore	Alicia Silverstone	Katie Holmes
Winona Ryder	Alyssa Milano		

Library of Congress Cataloging-in-Publication Data
Gaines, Ann.
     Britney Spears / Ann Graham Gaines.
        p. cm. — (A real-life reader biography)
     Includes index.
     Summary: A brief biography of the former Mouseketeer and popular young singer, Britney Spears.
     ISBN 1-58415-060-2
     1. Spears, Britney Juvenile literature. 2. Singers — United States Biography Juvenile literature.
[1. Spears, Britney. 2. Singers. 3. Women Biography.] I. Title. II. Series.
     ML3930.S713G35 2000
     782.42164'092—dc21
     [B]
                                                         99-38537
                                                           CIP

ABOUT THE AUTHOR: Ann Graham Gaines holds graduate degrees in American Civilization and Library and Information Science from the University of Texas at Austin. She has been a freelance writer for 18 years, specializing in nonfiction for children. She lives near Gonzales, Texas with her husband and their four children.

PHOTO CREDITS: cover: Fitzroy Barrett/Globe Photos; p. 4 courtesy Jive Records; p. 8, 15, 21, 31 Mark Allan/Globe Photos; p. 27 Henry McGee/Globe Photos; p. 30 Ron Davis/Shooting Star.

ACKNOWLEDGMENTS: The following story has been thoroughly researched, and to the best of our knowledge, represents a true story. Though we try to authorize every biography that we publish, for various reasons, this is not always possible. This story is neither authorized nor endorsed by Britney Spears.

Table of Contents

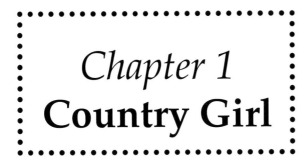

Chapter 1
Country Girl

In 1998, teenager Britney Spears became a pop star in what seemed like the blink of an eye. She seized the attention of the record industry when her very first single rocketed to the top of the charts. Then her album went platinum—meaning it sold one million copies—in just a few weeks. At 17, she looked like a sweet kid whose major interests were going to the beach, shopping and eating junk food. But interviewers who talked

In 1998, teenager Britney Spears became a pop star in what seemed like the blink of an eye.

to her found out that she is actually a very hard worker who is responsible for her own success. They also discovered that one key to her happiness is that she remains committed to her values and close to her family even while dedicating a great deal of attention to her career. It seems possible that she will remain a superstar for a long time because of her many talents, for Britney not only sings but also has experience acting and dancing.

Britney Jean Spears was born on December 2, 1981 to her mother, Lynne, and her father, Jamie. She is the second of three children. Her big brother, Bryan, is four years older than Britney, and her little sister, Jamie Lynn, is nine years younger than Britney.

The Spears are a close-knit family. They live in Kentwood,

Louisiana. Britney's mom teaches second grade. Her dad works in construction as a contractor, which means he is the boss of a construction crew. For the last few years, there has not been much construction work in the area in which they live, so he works in Memphis, Tennessee. But he comes home whenever he can.

The Spears spend a lot of time together, just hanging out. The kids get along well. Britney calls Bryan a laid-back country boy who loves football. He watches out for his sisters. Britney considers Jamie Lynn a wild child because she is full of personality and there's no telling what she'll do next. Her little sister is just like Britney in that she has loved to sing ever since she was very small. The Spears children also see their grandparents all the time.

Britney has experience singing, acting, and dancing.

Though Britney may look like a regular teenager, she has never lived her life as one. She has pursued an entertainment career since she was a young girl. Most of her school years were spent with a tutor, though she did attend a private school for awhile.

Britney loves it when her Granny, as she calls her, bakes pie.

Kentwood is a tiny town, with a population of less than two thousand people. It is located in Tangipahoa Parish (the state of Louisiana is broken up into parishes instead of counties). Kentwood sits in the eastern part of the state, just south of the Mississippi border. In this area, the countryside is beautiful, with gently rolling hills. Farms surround Kentwood. There's even one very special farm nearby that raises alligators! In many ways, Kentwood is a very Southern town. Life is slow-paced there. Residents speak with a drawl. They're soft-spoken and polite—children use "ma'am" and "sir" when they speak to grown-ups.

Kentwood is so small that it doesn't even have a junior high school. Children in grades seven

Britney's hometown of Kentwood, Louisiana is so small it doesn't even have a junior high school.

through twelve attend a single public high school. Kentwood has a few stores, a handful of restaurants—including Britney's favorite, a Sonic hamburger drive-in—and several churches. Britney thinks living in such a small town is both good and bad. Usually, she says, it's good to know everyone you see. But you don't get much privacy. Everybody knows your business. One thing she especially likes about Kentwood, though, is that from there it takes just an hour to get to New Orleans, one of the United States' most exciting cities. Tourists flock to New Orleans every year for Mardi Gras, with its colorful carnivals and parades. It is a lively city, famous for its music—just the kind of place you might imagine Britney would love.

Chapter 2
On Stage

From the time she was very small, Britney loved to perform. Offstage, she has said, she was quiet. But she would light up on stage. Laughing, her family remembers her at the age of three, dancing around, singing, and pretending her hairbrush was a microphone.

Britney has loved to perform since she was very small.

The Spears family attends a Baptist church faithfully. Britney often sang and appeared in pageants at church when she was as young as four years old. When she was still in elementary school, she started to enter talent shows, in which she sang and danced. For a time, she dreamed of becoming a gymnast. Britney stopped taking gymnastics lessons when she reached a point where, no matter how much she practiced, she could not learn an especially hard move. But she didn't let her failure break down her confidence. She kept seizing every opportunity to get up in front of an audience.

When Britney was eight, she heard that television's Disney Channel was going to launch a new version of *The Mickey Mouse Club*. According to Britney, her mom and dad have never been "stage parents." In other words, they never pushed her to perform. She has always been the one to decide what she wanted to do. But her parents have always supported her. So when she told them she wanted to go to Atlanta, Georgia, to audition for a part as a Mouseketeer on the show, they agreed to take her.

Although Britney did very well at her audition, she did not get chosen for the show. The man in charge of casting thought she was too young. But he did help her get a manager in a New York talent agency who helped her find plenty of other work as a child actress.

In the years that followed, Britney starred in some television commercials. In 1991, she also appeared in a play called *Ruthless* off-Broadway in New York City. The play was based on the 1956 horror film *The Bad Seed*. Britney played Tina, a ruthless little killer.

A New York talent agency helped Britney find work as a child actress.

This was an achievement that would make any actor proud. To be in this play, Britney moved with her mom to the Big Apple for a time.

For three years in a row, Britney also went to summer classes at the Professional Performing Arts School in New York City. This small public school specializes in training children with special talents for careers in music, dance and the theater.

When Britney was 11, she was finally offered a role as a Mouseketeer on *The Mickey Mouse Club*. Its cast included about twenty kids. There she got to know other people who would go on to become stars as teenagers, including Justin Timberlake and J. C. Chasez from 'N Sync. Appearing on *The Mickey Mouse Club* meant she lived for six months of every year in Orlando,

When Britney was 11, she was finally offered a role on *The Mickey Mouse Club*.

Florida. Only when a season wrapped (finished filming) would she return to Kentwood. She had no time for regular school. Children who appear on television shows attend school at home or go to classes taught by a tutor near a show's set.

Britney gained experience recording songs when she was a Mouseketeer. This helped when she finally did her own album.

Britney thought being a Mouseketeer was a lot of fun. The show was taped at Disney World. On it, she often sang and danced. The *Mickey Mouse Club* cast sometimes appeared live, putting on shows for audiences at

Britney was a Mouseketeer for two years, until the show was canceled.

Disney World. They also made records. Experience in a recording studio would later pay off in a big way for Britney.

Britney was a Mouseketeer for two years, until the show was canceled. This made her feel sad—but not too bad. Britney has always had a very healthy attitude about her career. Of course she likes to succeed. But she realizes that nobody in show business succeeds all the time. She just makes new plans when her old plans fall through.

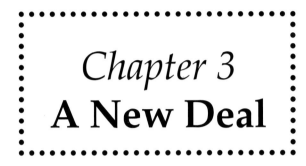

Chapter 3
A New Deal

After *The Mickey Mouse Club* ended, Britney returned home to Kentwood. She went back to being a regular student, attending a private school called Park Lane near her home. She liked school, especially hanging out with her friends. She enjoyed her first romance, with a boy named Reg. They went to the prom. But after a while, she felt "itchy." She was looking for a way to get back on stage. Wanting to help her find new

After *The Mickey Mouse Club* ended, Britney went back to being a regular student.

work, her father telephoned Larry Rudolph, a lawyer in New York City. He handles contracts for many singers. Rudolph suggested she think about a new career in pop music—light, entertaining music that was just then coming back into fashion. Britney loves pop, and she was delighted by his suggestion. Rudolph helped her arrange to make a demo, which is a sample song recorded in a studio.

When executives at Jive Records heard Britney's demo, they liked it so much they asked her to come to their offices to audition. Britney sang for Jive's business people in a conference room. "I was *so* nervous," she later said, describing the experience. "It's easy to sing in front of a thousand people, because you can't see their faces." It's different, she added, "[when] you go into a room, and there are ten people staring at you." She need not have worried. The Jive people thought she was fantastic. They loved both her voice and her motivation. They offered her a contract. She was then just 15 years old.

Jive believed that Britney's potential to sell records was so great that they hired Eric Foster White and Max Martin to produce her first album. These two are among the biggest names in the music industry today. White had worked with Whitney Houston, and Martin had helped the Backstreet Boys get started.

It took about a year and a half for Britney to make her first record and get it on the radio. The time passed very quickly for her. Although she went home to

Jive Records offered her a recording contract and hired two of the biggest names in the music industry to produce her first album.

Kentwood whenever she could—she says she always loves to get home, to see her doll collection and sleep in her own bed—she spent most of her time in and around the Jive offices in New York City. After she signed with Jive, she no longer went to a regular school, but got private lessons from tutors. She didn't have a lot of time for normal teenage things, like watching TV or dating.

From the time she made her record deal, she spent about six months in a recording studio. There she would listen to songs White and others thought she might want to include on her album. She also did some recording. Then Jive sent her on a trip to Sweden, where Max Martin lives and works. They hit it off right away. Martin played for her a demo of a song he had written called ...*Baby One More Time*, which she had never heard before. She loved it so much that she recorded it right away. Jive had planned for Britney and Martin to work on just two songs together. But Martin and his crew were so impressed with her, they came up with more and more songs they wanted to hear her sing. By the time she left Sweden, she'd recorded eight of the eleven songs that would go on her first album. She was so busy working in Sweden, she would later recall, that she never had

From the time Britney was small, she loved to get on stage and entertain. Here she is promoting her new album ...Baby One More Time.

a chance to play the part of a tourist and see any of the sights.

After she recorded that album, she made a video to go along with her first single. She got really involved in it, suggesting it tell a story about a bored schoolgirl daydreaming about making up with an old boyfriend. It was her idea, too, to have the dancers wear Catholic school uniforms and kneesocks.

In the meantime, Jive Records did all it could to make her first song a hit. Before the song ever played on the radio, Jive sent Britney on a tour of malls across the United States. This gave her more practice performing in front of a live audience. It also helped the nation's teenagers find out who she was. At the same time, Jive set up a Web site devoted to her. They advertised it by sending out postcards to members of many pop bands' fan clubs. They even paid for a special toll-free phone number so fans could call to listen to a recording of Britney singing.

When it came close to time for her first single to be released, Jive also sent her around to some of the most important radio stations in the country to meet disc jockeys and promote her record. At the same time, the company negotiated for another of her songs, *Soda Pop*, to be featured on TV's *Sabrina, the Teenage Witch*. Jive was doing everything possible to bring Britney's music to young listeners.

Britney went on a tour of malls all across the United States.

Chapter 4
...Baby One More Time

Britney's debut single, *...Baby One More Time*, was released on September 30, 1998. This was a tremendously exciting time for Britney. The first time she heard her song on the radio, she says, "It was the best feeling."

Every week, *Billboard* magazine publishes charts that tell the music industry which songs are getting played the most by disc jockeys on the radio. In its first week on the air, Britney's song got played more than any other new release. Within three weeks, a huge number of fans were calling radio stations to request her song. All through the fall, ...*Baby One More Time* sped up the charts. At the same time, her video made it onto television, where it also received top ratings.

In November, Jive announced that Britney was going to go on tour with 'N Sync. Britney was the only guest artist on the tour, and appeared with them for three months. She remembers the tour as having been scary at first, because "it was already out there that a *girl* was opening up for 'N Sync. I'd walk out there and my first two performances, they were like, 'Booooo.' [But] once I'd start performing they'd go crazy."

Britney's seventeenth birthday, on December 2, 1998, got noted in

Britney went on tour with 'N Sync for three months.

newspapers all over the country. On January 11, 1999, millions of people watched her performance at the American Music Awards. Her first album, also named ...*Baby One More Time*, was released the very next day, on January 12. It was also a huge hit, selling more than one hundred thousand copies the very first week it hit the stores.

Britney's success made her a celebrity. Positive reviews of both the single and the album appeared, it seemed, everywhere. She was featured in many teen magazines like *Teen People* and *Jump*. Interviewers liked her upbeat personality and the fact that she seemingly never had anything negative to say. *Seventeen* magazine featured her in a makeover. She appeared on the cover of *Rolling Stone*. It really hit home, however, that she had hit the big time when she got invited to appear on *The Tonight Show with Jay Leno* and the *Late Show with David Letterman.* Such appearances meant she was starting to get recognized on the street, although she counted herself lucky that her fame had not yet reached a point where she found it hard to go out in public.

Below, Britney arrives at the Ed Sullivan Theatre in New York City for the Late Show With David Letterman.

Britney had so many fans, though, that she was ready to headline—to be the lead performer on a tour. In April, Jive Records announced that Britney would kick off her own tour on June 28, 1999. When Jive made the announcement, her album was Number One in the United States. By summer, in fact, Britney's album had gone quadruple platinum, which means it had sold more than four million copies. Britney made history when she became the first new female artist ever to have her first single and her first album *both* in the number one slot on the charts the very same week.

Britney was scheduled to hold 48 concerts in 48 different cities—including places like New York and Los Angeles—in just a little over two months. On April 26, Jive released her second single, called *Sometimes*. Some singers struggle for years to succeed—but Britney Spears had become a famous singing star less than six months after her first single had appeared.

By summer 1999, Britney's first album had sold more than four million copies.

Chapter 5
The Future

Britney is very proud of her first album. She loves having fans who can sing all the words to her songs. She talks of having a long and successful singing career. "I want to be big all around the world," she says, simply summing up her goals. She dreams of one day making it in the movies, too, like her idol Whitney Houston. She especially likes it when journalists compare her to Madonna, whom

Britney still dreams of being a big star. She wants a movie career, too.

Britney admires as much for her versatility as for her singing ability.

Britney is willing to work extremely hard to try to become a star of the stature of Madonna. She not only is dedicated to practicing her singing and dancing, but she dedicates herself to promoting her work. She is friendly to fans. She grants many interviews.

Britney performed at the World Music Awards on May 20, 1999.

But she also knows that fame can be fleeting. So she plans to continue to take courses from tutors and get her high school diploma. Eventually she will go on to college, she says. "I definitely want something to fall back on and to have something to look forward to," she told an interviewer.

In March 1999, Britney signed a contract with Columbia Tristar to appear in three episodes of Dawson's Creek. Her new deal with Columbia Tristar also has them developing a new show just for her.

Britney has been the driving force behind her career since she was young. Her parents have never pushed her, but they have supported her aspirations.

To others who share her dreams, she offers encouragement. When someone jokingly asked her whether she thought he should pursue his goal of becoming a singer, she gave a serious reply. "I say go for it. Just believe and work hard." Anyone with a talent, she believes, should display it.

Chronology

- Born December 2, 1981 in Kentwood, Louisiana; mother: Lynne; father: Jamie
- Started to perform on stage at age four, even before enrolling in school
- At age eight, auditioned for role on the Disney Channel's *Mickey Mouse Club*
- Appeared in off-Broadway play, *Ruthless*, in 1991
- At age 11, given role on *The Mickey Mouse Club*
- *The Mickey Mouse Club* is canceled when Britney is 14, and she returns home to go to school
- Signed by Jive Records, 1997
- Single, ...*Baby One More Time*, released September 30, 1998
- Starts touring as the opening act for 'N Sync, November 1998
- Album, also named ...*Baby One More Time*, released January 12, 1999
- March 1999, signs contract with Columbia Tristar to appear on several episodes of Dawson's Creek, and to develop a new TV show just for her.
- Jive releases Britney's second single, *Sometimes,* April 26, 1999
- Britney sets off on own tour on June 28, 1999, planning to sing in 48 cities

Index